REMEMBERING WHY I TEACH

Letters From My Students

INSPIRED BY TRUE LETTERS FROM
CHILDREN TO THEIR TEACHERS

MIGUEL HERNANDEZ

Copyright © 2020 by Miguel Hernandez

Letters From My Students

Quantity sales special discounts are available on quantity purchases by corporations, associations, and others. For details, contact the publisher at the address above.

Orders by U.S. trade bookstores and wholesalers. Email info@BeyondPublishing.net

The Beyond Publishing Speakers Bureau can bring authors to your live event. For more information or to book an event contact the Beyond Publishing Speakers Bureau speak@BeyondPublishing.net

The Author can be reached directly at BeyondPublishing.net

Manufactured and printed in the United States of America distributed globally by BeyondPublishing.net

BEYOND
PUBLISHING

New York | Los Angeles | London | Sydney

ISBN Hardcover: 978-1-637920-44-2

Table of Contents

The Letters

Prologue

My work as an educator, teacher and administrator over these many years has turned hundreds of teachers and students into my best friends. I have cried with them, laughed with them and learned about life from them. I love them all.

A career in education comes with a personal cost. So many times, we wonder what life would look like if we had a 9-5 job with clear expectations, working with adults who did important things. And of course, made more money than a teacher usually makes.

Most of us don't wonder very long. We have come to discover there are few investments more significant than the work of raising a young human. We become father and mother, counselor, teacher, encourager and protector for the earth's most valuable natural resource—our children. The future of our world is chattering away in classrooms around the globe. I would rather do nothing else in the world.

Letters to My Students began as a different book. I wrote my first words in the weeks leading up to the world-wide pandemic that has changed the planet. The book was to be about becoming more effective teachers and raising test scores and other such matters. As classrooms became virtual and teachers could no longer feel the live presence of their children, I realized test scores would have to wait until later. Overnight, the pandemic had made teachers the most important people in our society. I needed to go there.

This is a time when we remember why we teach. Whether in a classroom for the first time or having taught for 30 years, it is a career of stories and letters. You are part of a community of adults who, every day, change the lives of children. You are creating memories and moments that affect them for a lifetime. I want you to remember that.

Letters To My Students is a collection of just a few of these stories. You may laugh or you may cry. Just never forget why you do this. We teachers are bigger than a pandemic and are nurturing the hope for a better tomorrow.

I love you all,

Miguel

Letters

1. You believed in me, when no one else did. (This is why you should believe in others.)

2. The effort you put into your job inspired me. (This is why you should inspire others.)

3. Your desire to make the world a better place changed me.

4. You taught me the dignity that comes from discipline.

5. You showed me I can achieve more than I originally think, always.

6. You taught me to dream about my future.

7. Thank you for being genuine.

8. Thank you for your patience, and for not embarrassing me in front of my friends with my learning disability. (This is why you have to always be patient with others.)

9. Thank you for your bravery in confronting injustice. (This is why you have to stand up for what is right.)

10. You taught me what it means to trust someone. (This is why you should trust others.)

11. You spoke to my heart. Thank you. (This is why you should look to touch hearts.)

12. You acknowledged my talents. (This is why you should do that for others.)

13. You opened my mind. (This is why you should open the minds of others.)

14. You saved my life. (This is how you respond when someone is struggling.)

15. Thank you for listening to me. (This is why you have to listen.)

16. Thank you for helping me explore. (This is what it means to explore.)

17. Thank you for asking me questions. (This is why you should ask questions.)

18. Thank you for showing me life is a journey. (This is why you should think of life as a journey)

19. Thank you for accepting my apology. (This is why you should accept apologies and forgive.)

20. Thank you for making me laugh. (This is why humor is so important.)

You believed In me, when no one else did

Dear Mr. M.,

I remember when I started in your class, and I had to walk the eight blocks to and from school, at 6 in the morning, carrying a backpack that must have weighed a million pounds. I remember the first time you saw me when I walked in, you said, "That looks heavy!" The way you said it made me laugh, and it somehow made me feel better. I remember how nervous I was to meet you, as you spoke to me for the first time. I remember the look of worry on your face when you found out I was from a single-parent household. I remember my first day of school, and how you sat down with me after school and gave me advice on how to deal with bullies, so I wouldn't get my lunch money taken, or even worse, get beaten up. I remember my first picture day, and how you helped me put on my backpack and then asked if I wanted to get ice cream later that day.

I remember the day I told you I was autistic. I know now you already knew, but I remember how you cried with me, and how it still makes me cry. I remember how you made me promise not to hold it against you if people made fun of me. I remember that you taught me to be myself, and not to let others walk all over me. I remember that you let me know that bullies can make other people more aware of themselves, and that they shouldn't make fun of others for things they have no control over. I remember all the laughs and jokes, the snow days, the awful PE teachers, and of course, you always letting me have the last piece of cake when you brought it in. I remember how you supported me through high school, when everyone said I wouldn't go to college, and when others would criticize me. I remember your influence in helping me succeed in high school.

I remember how you believed in me, and how you believed in my potential. Thank you for all you have done for me and all you have taught me. I remember all the times I cried when I got back from school, because of what I had learned.

I remember how you believed in me, and how you always believed in me. Thank you for all you have done for me. You believed in me, when no one else did. Your ability to know what I needed to realize my gifts was far and away the greatest gift I could have ever been given. You showed me that it is not just enough to have gifts, you also need to believe in your gifts. I believe in mine more, thanks to you.

You've always been there for me. I could always go to you for advice or any kind of help I may need.

You are a part of who I am today. You know that I am going to be okay without you, and that I will always have a space in my heart for that belief. I will miss you terribly, but if I believe in myself even half as much as you believed in me, I know I will succeed.

Your student,

Latisha

Dear Latisha,

Your words have moved me deeply. I am grateful for the countenance and grace you showed as a student. More than that, you have made my job easy. You have been eager to take the belief I felt in you and believe in yourself. Whether you know it or not, you were believing in yourself all along.

What does it mean to believe in someone?

Believe in someone with an open heart, a forgiving mind, and an open hand. When you open yourself to another person, you are opening yourself to all that they have to offer.

In your darkest moments, you can choose to stand with, stand up for, and speak out for your classmates, like you might have felt I did for you. We need more of you, people who know what it means to believe in something believing in others.

When you open yourself to others, you give them a home. When you speak up for others, you become a powerful leader. When you have the courage to believe in someone, you spread your voice far beyond the boundaries of your classroom and far beyond the school walls.

You are setting a powerful example for young girls and young women, showing them that they are more than the name they are given, the person they are treated as, or the stereotypes society has placed on them. You are fighting for your dignity. You are believing in yourself.

Latisha, you are young, but you are wise beyond your years. You will be going to college one day. What will your focus be? Why are you going to college? What do you want to do when you graduate?

Once you answer these questions, do not give up on yourself. Keep striving to grow in your self-esteem and self-love. The world needs you.

I will see you in the hallways and on the playground. I am sure I will see you giving your best, like all of us. Keep your confidence; you have a bright future.

I will always be here for you. Thank you for all you have given me.

Sincerely,

Mr. M.

The effort you put into your job inspired me

Dear Mr. M.,

You have inspired me in so many ways. I have never seen someone put so much effort into teaching. Every morning, I would come into your classroom looking forward to seeing what would cover the board. Some mornings, you had been there since seven in the morning, using your skills as an artist to create a comic book-like presentation with incredible illustrations on the white board. It was so amazing and made learning so much more enjoyable. The way you taught us history was above and beyond what I could have expected in my wildest imagination. You inspired me to do more in all of my classes. You inspired me to do what I couldn't imagine was possible. And the way that you put effort into things seemed so natural and effortless. It was just a pure extension of who you are. I honestly didn't know you were actually an artist. It's so ironic that you didn't want to be "seen" as an artist. The way that you had your art projects set up and displayed throughout the classroom was an incredible example to me of the type of artist that you are. I hope you know how much you've inspired me.

You had the humblest approach to teaching. It was as if this is what you were meant to do, and that inspired me every day. I actually thought about how excited I was to go to your class after school, because I wanted that feeling of inspiration. I don't know how you did it!

I am so grateful to you for your amazing teaching.

On Monday, I was thinking about all the moments I had in your class and how I've never had anything like that before. I am so thankful to have had such a unique experience, such an amazing teacher. I can't believe I will never have that chance again.

Most importantly, you taught me that art is a path to your soul; no matter what you are doing, you can make it artistic. I think I can speak for all of us. We felt that, and we knew we were able to express who we were in your classroom. That was inspiring. It inspired me to be the best person I could be. You inspired us to get inspired. I felt like I was able to express my biggest, innermost feelings, when you would set aside time for us to journal for five minutes before class started. It made me so much more focused for your lesson. It's like we all had a secret moment in a private room. There was something that connected us, that we had to share with the world through this work of art we had just made.

And then, we were inspired for the whole class. Because of you, and the incredible effort you brought to your job.

Sincerely,

Thomas

Dear Thomas,

Your words have moved me. It makes me so happy to know that I have served as an inspiration to you, and that my efforts as a teacher have not gone unnoticed. I am convinced that you could answer many of the important questions about why it is so important that you always put in that extra effort. But here are a few:

I want you to always remember that you have been given a gift in your voice. Your voice is unique. You are special. You have a unique gift, and that gift is of great importance. Even though it may seem to others that you have no talent, you should not question your own gift. You have given me many great lessons and have provided much food for thought. I would like you to know that I am extremely grateful for your gift. This is the key to putting in the extra effort - you want to feed those gifts and be thankful for those gifts.

In order to continue to learn and grow, you must always remain thankful for the gift that you have been given. You must always remember the gifts that others have given you. The gift of laughter and playfulness. The gift of time and patience. The gift of friendship. The gift of encouragement. The gift of unconditional love. The gift of your great compassion for others. The gift of your wonderful sense of humor. The gift of your joyful voice. The gift of your sense of caring. The gift of your wonderful smile. And so much more. You must be thankful for all of your gifts. There is so much that you must continue to learn. You must always think about how you can best use your gifts. Do not be afraid to learn new things.

This excitement is what will motivate you to put in that extra effort and be an inspiration to others. Every day that I came to teach class, believe it or not, I came with an open mind and an open heart, ready to learn new things.

The essence of inspiration is to continue to feel excitement about life, about things that you have always wanted to learn about, but just didn't know enough to get started. And, to continue to be inspired about the things that you are already learning. This takes effort.

But it is effortless effort.

The essence of inspiration is to continue to discover and appreciate what is really important in life. If you have that kind of inspiration, then you will want to find ways to put more into your life, as well as learn how to live more fully, in every moment, and for each person. You must allow your gifts to help others. And remember, your teachers always, always, gave you so much, and you must share your gifts with others.

Yours truly,

Mr. M.

Your desire to make the world a better place changed me

Dear Mr. M.,

You had the most infectious desire to make the world a better place. I am so grateful for seeing how you took that desire and made it into your everyday. I knew I wanted to make the world a better place, so I took every day of being in your class as a lesson in how to live the life I wanted to live. You inspired me to be kind to every kid at recess, including and especially the kids I didn't like the best.

I remember the story you told us about your childhood best friend. I remember feeling like it would be impossible for me to ever have something like that happen in my life. I remember you saying how you met your best friend, how he was someone you always thought was silly and not at all someone who would make a good friend. Then one day, you saw that he was crying on the playground, and you went and put your arms around him, and offered him comfort. Then, he became your best friend. Even though that never happened to me, I know it was the right thing, and shows me how you were dedicated to making the world a better place.

You taught me that a smile is the easiest way to get along with anyone. Your smile was almost always as genuine as it was beautiful, and your laugh matched it. When you told a joke, it was guaranteed to be one everyone would laugh at. When you told us your jokes, it was even more guaranteed. You taught me how to think before I spoke, and to always be sure of what I was saying before I said it. Whenever I saw you, you always had a ready smile and a cheerful greeting. Everyone just knew that you would give them whatever they needed, and they always ended up knowing that, too. You made everybody feel like they were a part of your class, and you made them feel like it was their place to be there, too. That's what makes you special. You are special. With even these small things, I saw your desire to change the world, and it changed me.

Thank you for all that you did to make me a better person. I really needed every minute I was in your class, and I carry those lessons forward into the world.

Sincerely,

Caroline

Dear Caroline,

Thank you for this sweet and heartfelt note. Here is why you always should desire to make the world a better place. The world needs all of us to make it what it is. It truly is up to us, the world that we and everyone else will live in. How can we expect the world to become a better place by accident? We can't. We, ourselves, need to be the ones to make it all happen. We make it happen by paying attention to our world, to our everyday. Our lives are so tightly wrapped up in the people and things we love. Those things make our lives even richer, so we should pay attention to them as much as we do to ourselves. By paying attention, we are acknowledging who we are in the world. We are acknowledging our individual and unique gifts. We are claiming our place in this world. We are making a difference.

You should always want to make the world a better place, because it will always become a better place for you. You are special, because you are on this planet right now. You matter. That is something that everyone needs to hear. We need to remember that we are all unique beings in this world. We are not just the sum of our bodies and the skills we can use. We are much more than that. What our lives are made up of is what is important. We are not defined by our physical make-up. If we are living a life of purpose and love and joy, we are a much, much greater being than we ever were when we were living in fear and hate and anger. We are everything we could be if we live with integrity. We are human beings. We matter.

Whenever you can, you can use your uniqueness. I want you to use it in service. We need people like you in this world who are not afraid of other people's feelings or their needs. There are some who are afraid of what others might say about them if they do what they want to do, so they get pushed back in line. We need more people who are not afraid. We need you to help change our world. If we don't change our world, the world will change us. We need you to help us change it.

Caroline, let your unique talents be used in service to others. I know how much it means to you to help. I know how much you love to help other people. When you learn about all that the world has to offer, you'll be tempted to ignore it, because it is hard to think of more than your family and your neighborhood. For you to have more power than those around you, you will need to help change things. You need to make the world better. You have so much power. Use it for good. Use it for yourself. Use it for the world. Use it to make it a better place.

I'm glad I got to be your teacher.

Sincerely,

Mr. M.

You taught me the dignity that comes from discipline

Dear Mr. M.,

I am so glad I had you for all of third grade. Though I learned so much in your class, and carry with me so many lessons from your life, the thing I learned the most was that having a strong sense of self-worth comes from putting in effort.

I remember after I failed a test, I was feeling really bad about myself. It was only a spelling quiz, but still, I wanted to get a perfect score. I was crying. You pulled me aside, and you asked me how much I had studied for the test. I didn't want to answer, because all I had done to prepare was eat ice cream and play video games. So, I just said, "not a lot." You told me very kindly that one way to build up self-esteem, the word you said was "dignity", is to work really hard to achieve our goals.

Your words touched my heart, Mr. M. I knew they were very true. I imagined how hard you had worked to get to the place you were, as a teacher. All the things you had to do. All the tests you had to take and all the challenges you needed to face. I always thought people just got to where they were as adults as if by magic, but you really helped me to see all the hard work that goes into you getting there. I realized I would have to work hard, and then, I wouldn't feel so bad if I didn't get the grade I wanted. I would be more likely to get the grade I wanted, and if I didn't, I'd at least know I did my very best, which is a source of dignity.

That is my new favorite word, "dignity".

Without it, I would still be crying about that spelling test. Instead, I am studying hard and excited to be going into fourth grade. I will take the lessons I learned this year into next year. It has also showed me that others who are struggling need to be respected, because in that struggle, there is so much dignity. They are working hard for what they want to accomplish, and I need to respect that. We all deserve dignity, and we all deserve to support one another on the long, hard road to making that happen.

Third grade wasn't easy, let me tell ya. It was full of so many difficult days. But you helped me to remember that I was working for something much bigger than I could have ever imagined. I needed that discipline you instilled in me. I am so grateful for it. I am so thankful for you.

I wonder what experiences you had that made you learn about dignity. Because when you spoke that to me, I knew it came from your heart.

Thank you for teaching me about "dignity" and so much more.

Your student,

Mickey

Dear Mickey,

Thank you for opening up to me that day. It is never easy to do poorly on a test, and yes, we all have to go through it to get better and find our way. I am glad my words spoke to you. Dignity is one of the best things we can have as human beings, and it comes from being honest, straightforward, and always giving everything our absolute best. I know you will have that throughout your whole life, and your strong work ethic will guide you wherever you need to go.

Where do you want to go? This is a question that you can answer with your dignity. You know that you are worth every step you take, so what steps are you going to take? The steps we take end up defining the life we live, and if you take steps full of dignity, you will lead a life of dignity.

You have learned so much this year. For not only a third grader, but for a human being. It makes me proud to know you.

You asked me what experiences I have had that taught me about dignity. I learned when my mother was going through cancer treatment. I spent the summer caring for her. She had to lie in bed for most of the day, to keep food down, and to take her medicine. I got used to it, and we had a wonderful time talking, doing schoolwork, and playing with my dogs. Every day, we called each other, and she would ask me if I was still with her. She was always so happy to hear my voice.

We laughed and cried together. Even though my mother was very sick, she was always trying to keep me laughing. When she was in pain and it hurt her so bad, she would tell me to make her laugh. She was a great writer, and many of the stories she told me about our family were funny, so I would try to remember them when I needed to feel better.

We made a video and watched it together every night when she couldn't sleep. Sometimes, she would come to my room and just sit in my bed and hug me. She had been sick for a long time, and she was getting tired of fighting.

One night, she was having a hard time breathing, and I knew it. I begged her to please go to the hospital. She was stubborn and said she didn't have time, and she would try to sleep and take her medicine. She stayed, and she went to sleep. I was just so scared. I couldn't make her go to the hospital, and I couldn't wake her. I couldn't give her the comfort I knew she needed. So, I called the ambulance and told them what I knew. I was crying and begging her to come with me. She wouldn't wake up, so I knew she was gone. But she had left this world where she wanted, in her home, in a dignified way. I was sad, but I respected her for that.

I took the phone and wept into it, calling for the ambulance. When I got to the hospital, I sat down in the hallway and sobbed into my hand. An officer came over to me and asked me if I needed help. I took that opportunity to tell him that my mother had died. I wanted him to know. I wanted him to say something, even if I was going to make him cry, too. He looked at me and said, "I am so sorry, I am sure she was an incredible woman." And because I knew it was true, it made me feel so much better.

So, please, live the best life you can, love every moment, and never give up your dignity!

Your teacher,

Mr. M.

You showed me I can achieve more than I originally thought

Dear Mrs. Robinson,

It's been a long time since we last spoke; I'm sure you wouldn't even recognize me now. Maybe that's a good thing. The girl I was when I met you is not someone I am particularly fond of. She was pretty rude, distant, and sometimes, downright mean. I'd like to believe I am not like that anymore. I'd like to get as far away from that girl as I can in every possible respect.

I know you and I were not particularly close. Our relationship was mostly 'hellos' and 'goodbyes', with the occasional request for a bathroom break sandwiched in between. I'm sure you must know, though, that this was a far healthier relationship than I had with any other teacher in the building. I took a fair amount of pleasure from driving your colleagues up the wall. Sarcastic replies, frequent tardiness and absence, arguments, sporadic fights, homework turned in late—if at all, and a churlish devotion to maintaining a C/D average was all par for the course. Many of them openly disliked me, and frankly, I don't blame them.

It's not that I disliked any of them, believe it or not. Honestly, I was hardly aware of their existence. I hated the seventh grade for a number of reasons, but the teachers weren't one of them. The summer before seventh grade, my mom met a man named Bill at a

neighborhood barbecue. She and Bill hit it off rather quickly. As he came over more and more frequently, it felt like my mom was around less and less. She had always had rather terrible taste in men, and I knew that Bill would be no different.

I'll spare you the details, but things got pretty ugly at home. My mom and I barely spoke. When we did, it was only to snap at each other. Bill tried to befriend me, but I had no interest in getting to know him. I knew he'd be gone soon enough. School became just another outlet for my frustrations. One teacher tried to talk to me about any "problems" or "difficulties" I might be facing at home, but I refused to engage. I had no interest in discussing my feelings or my struggles with anyone.

Midway through September, you wrapped up a lesson on mitosis with the announcement that you would be taking a week off of school to visit your sister. You looked me right in the eye and asked me if I could be the one to take care of Cheddar while you were gone. I must say I was shocked you asked me. Just two days prior, I had "accidentally" spilled a bottle of dye on a poster of the periodic table and "forgotten" to tell you about it. I immediately agreed to babysit our chinchilla pal. After class, you showed me how to fill his water bottle, when and how to feed him, and how to change his bedding. You concluded the tutorial by saying, "This is a big responsibility, Fiona. I'm trusting you to take care of something that means a lot to me. Alright?"

I spent the next week walking on eggshells. Constantly slipping out of my other classes to check on Cheddar. I fed, watered, and changed his bedding diligently. I sat with him between classes and stroked his fur. I've always liked animals better than people, and Cheddar was no exception. I like to think we had a calming effect on each other. I didn't get in a single fight that week.

When you came back, you thanked me for taking such good care of your friend. The next day, I found a small package on my desk containing a magnet with a picture of a chinchilla that read "Keep your ~chinchilla~ up!" and a thank you note signed 'Cheddar'.

You taught me the most important lesson I have ever learned about trust. That week, I discovered how powerfully transformative it can be to have someone trust you, put their faith in you, and how good it can feel to make sure that trust is kept. I spent the rest of the year making sure I earned the trust that you handed me so freely. Thank you for taking a chance on me. Your trust was a gift I did not deserve, but desperately needed.

Sincerely,

Fiona

P.S. Ten years later, Bill is still with us, and he's one of my favorite people. I suppose even a blind chinchilla finds a nut every once in a while.

***

Dear Fiona,

I am so thrilled to hear that Cheddar and I had a positive impact. Junior high is a tough time for many people, but it sounds as though you had a particularly rough go of it. Sometimes, our circumstances get the better of us. I understand why you may want to distance yourself from some of your past behaviors, but please do not shun the girl that you were. She was dealing with a lot of tough problems and doing the best she could.

I have been teaching for twenty-two years now. I have seen students of every kind pass through my doors. Not one of them has been undeserving of empathy or basic respect. From our brief conversations and observing you over the first few weeks of school,

I could tell you were bright, sensitive, and struggling. I have always found solace in my animal friends, and I had hoped that you would as well. I never doubted that you would put your best foot forward to take care of Cheddar. The two of you appeared to be fast friends from the moment you claimed the seat next to his cage. And you did not strike me as the type to let a friend down.

I believe the old adage goes "trust is hard to earn and easy to lose." While I agree that a violation of trust can be damaging, I have found that trusting in the goodwill of others often brings that goodwill to the fore. Your letter has brought me renewed faith in this belief. Thank you.

We teachers rarely get to find out how our students are doing once they leave our classrooms, and I cannot tell you what a treat it is to hear that you are doing well. Thank you so much for sharing this story with me. You've made my week!

Best Regards,

Mrs. Robinson

P.S. I should note, Cheddar was a remarkably picky chinchilla when it came to people, but he took to you within minutes. So, it's safe to say he deemed you trustworthy as well.

You taught me to dream about my future

Dear Mrs. Tierney,

Thank you for being such a fun and energetic teacher! I knew that your class was going to be really fun when I saw your map of America with all of the stickers showing the states that you visited. I can't believe you have been to Texas! I love traveling and I have always wanted a map like that! I also really liked the pictures and decorations you put around the classroom. The whale and dinosaur bones were really cool. The pictures you took in California were my favorite. I love the beach, and you took some really pretty shots of the sunset there!

You are my favorite teacher, because you let us have class outside all the time and took us on adventures. I know they were just walks in the woods, but I really enjoyed getting to be outside. You are the only teacher I have ever had who wanted to have class outside. Now, I can have class outside while I Zoom, but it's not the same. I miss hearing you use the acorn whistles to call us back inside. I have a lot of acorns in my backyard, and I am trying to learn how to use them as whistles. I can almost do it!

I also wanted to thank you for teaching us about the ocean. I had no idea that so much of the ocean has not been explored yet. It would be so cool to find a new creature in the ocean. When I grow up, I want to work on a boat or a submarine now because of you. That way I can work outside every day and discover new places and animals. Thank you for teaching me to love exploring!

Thank you,

Caleb

***

Dear Caleb,

It is so lovely to hear from you! I can't tell you how much I miss seeing you and your classmates every day. Zoom certainly is not the same. Please know I am sending you a virtual hug!

It is so important to remain curious about the world and our place in it. One of the reasons I enjoy having class outside is because I believe nature fosters that curiosity. Winter is coming soon, so try to get as many outdoor classes in as you can before it gets too cold. See if your parents would be willing to get you a disposable camera. Start documenting your adventures now. I can tell you from experience you will be so glad to have those memories captured on film and paper when you're older.

I'm so glad you want to pursue a career exploring our oceans. You are such a smart and talented kid; I can't wait to see what amazing things you discover!

If you need any assistance with acorn whistling, do let me know. I was about your age when I learned how to do it myself. :) I hope you have an excellent school year. Please keep in touch!

All good wishes,

Mrs. Tierney

You inspired me to be authentic

Dear Ms. Carter,

You are easily the funniest teacher I have ever had. You approached every day, every class, every topic, every assignment with a sense of humor. I truly do not know how you were able to be so upbeat every day. You never seemed to get tired! None of my other teachers have come close to being as funny and entertaining as you. I always left your classroom feeling better about myself and more optimistic. And I don't think that had anything to do with algebra.

Your math jokes of the day always made everyone in the class smile. My personal favorite was, "You know why seven eight nine? It is important to eat three square meals a day!" I thought it was a very clever twist on a well-known joke. I think the most popular one was, "Why is it sad that parallel lines have a great deal in common? Because they will never meet." I'm really curious if you came up with all of those jokes, or is there, like, a math teacher joke handbook???

I thought it was absolutely hilarious when you came into class on Pi Day dressed as a giant apple pie. I can't believe you wore the costume all day. You made us all laugh and all of our friends and other teachers, too. I know some of the other teachers had pi counting

contests and had their classes do pi arts and crafts, but you took it to another level. Next year, I think all the other math teachers should follow your lead and show up as different flavored pies. Or you could have a pi/pie costume contest with the winner getting a pie!

I know that your attitude and sense of humor was really helpful to a lot of kids in the class. A couple of my friends who have always hated math started to enjoy it in your class. I know one used to get really bad anxiety whenever he took a math test or did math homework. Like, so bad he needs extended time for tests. Or at least, he used to. Whenever he was starting to panic over a problem, you always managed to calm him down and show him that he really did know how to do it. I could hear you cracking jokes from a few rows over. It usually only took a few tries before he went from the verge of tears to full on belly-laughing.

You clearly have a gift for comedy, and I am so glad that you use it to help students like me learn and conquer problems we didn't believe we were capable of taking on. Your jokes always made intimidating math problems seem a little less scary and the world a little bit happier. My grandmother passed away before school one day while I was your student and I spent all day crying. You didn't know why I was so upset, and I was too sad to talk about it, but I could tell you tried extra hard to make me smile during that class anyways. It really meant a lot to me that you tried, even though I couldn't tell you how much I appreciated it at the time.

Thank you for being an amazingly funny and kind teacher. You helped all of us so much, both with math and in recognizing how important a good sense of humor can be. I'm afraid I have probably forgotten a lot of the math that you taught me, but I know I will never forget what an incredible difference a well-timed joke can make.

Thank you!

Tanya

***

Dearest Tanya,

It is so lovely to hear from you and such a gift to receive a letter as kind as yours. Thank you for taking the time to tell me how I have impacted you and your classmates. I am so sorry to hear about your grandmother and so happy that I was able to help you in your grief, in some small way. While I love math as deeply as pi is long, I must concur with you: in life, a good sense of humor will likely serve you better than an in-depth knowledge of algebra. What good is it to understand how the world works at the price of our humanity?

I hope you will take this appreciation for humor with you as you move through life.

Take your newfound appreciation for humor and be sure to spread it. It's dark out there for a lot of people. It will always be worthwhile to bring a little light into the room. You will also notice that happy, socially well-nourished people are a lot more productive than those who are expected to work like robots. Too often, the world pushes us to forget that we are human in the name of increasing productivity. Rather ironic, isn't it?

You are a wonderfully clever and kind girl, and I know you will go very far in whatever direction you choose to travel. I hope you take your marvelous sense of humor along for the ride. Words are powerful. Attitude is powerful. Your presence is powerful. You are capable of changing the lives of the people around you for the better, just by offering them a bit of your own good humor.

I cannot reveal the source of my jokes ;), but I am absolutely pitching a pie costume contest for next year's pie day. Frankly, I am disappointed in myself for not thinking of that!

Sincerely,

Ms. Carter

Thank you looking past my learning disability

Dear Mrs. Wright,

Thank you for accepting my apology. I really did not mean to break the computer, but I know that I need to take responsibility for my actions. When we started our magnet lab, you told us not to touch anything until you gave us all the instructions. I was really excited and started playing with the magnets before you finished giving the instructions. One of the instructions was to not put magnets near electronics, because they are bad for them. I did not know that about magnets. I had already put a magnet on a computer monitor to see if it would stick. The magnet was only on there for a minute, but that was enough time for the magnet to break it. I was so scared when the screen would not turn on right no matter what I did. I felt awful for letting you down and for breaking something that did not belong to me. Thank you for not yelling at me. I think I definitely would have cried a lot more if you had yelled at me.

I want to help pay for the damage. My mom said that she will pay me to do extra chores around the house, and I can use the money to pay for the computer screen. I do not know how much a computer screen costs. Please let me know how much the screen costs, and I will make sure that I get you that much as soon as possible.

Thank you, again, for being so nice about this. The scariest part was telling you about the screen, because I really don't want you to be mad at me. You are my favorite teacher, and I should have listened to your instructions before I started playing with the magnets.

Thank you,

Marin

Dear Marin,

Thank you for apologizing and owning up to your mistake so quickly. I know it can be really scary to acknowledge our mistakes, especially when we run the risk of disappointing someone. It is so important to both hold ourselves accountable and remember that everyone makes mistakes. That way, we can address our missteps freely and ensure that others feel comfortable doing the same.

I know you would never intentionally damage school property and that you feel terrible about breaking the computer monitor. It says a lot about your character that you brought the problem to my attention, instead of leaving me to find the broken computer later. Thank you for being courageous and honest. Please know that I would never yell at you over a mistake. I want everyone in my classroom to feel comfortable coming forward when something goes wrong. I believe that mutual respect and trust are fundamental to a well-functioning society (and classroom!), and that people need to feel safe if you want them to contribute at their full potential. I hope that you continue to feel safe bringing mistakes or any other issues to my attention.

If you take anything away from this, I hope it is an understanding of the importance of accountability and forgiveness (well... maybe the importance of following directions, too;)). Please tell your mother that you are neither expected nor required to pay for the damage to the computer monitor. The monitor in question was dreadfully old and well overdue to be replaced. Thank you for being such an engaged, honest, and curious learner. We need more like you.

Thank you,

Mrs. Wright

Thank you for your bravery in confronting injustice

Dear Mrs. Crawley,

Thank you for being the best third grade teacher ever. You are very smart about a lot of things and really good at teaching them to us. My favorite things to learn about were history and science (and also gym). I think I want to be a scientist when I grow up now. I wanted you to be my teacher again this year, but my mom says that you only teach third graders. She is helping me write this letter. I bet you already guessed that, because you know I am dyslexic.

That is another reason you are the best teacher ever. You always spent extra time with me during reading groups and helped me during spelling tests. I used to feel really embarrassed because the tests took a really long time for me. You made me feel better because you let me take my time and cheered me on when I got it right. You also didn't tell any of my friends about my dyslexia. I don't want anyone to know about it (except for teachers, because they have to), and you always made sure that my friends didn't hear us talk. I saw Carter ask you why you were helping me on a history test, and you told him that some of the questions on my test were blurry. I thought that was very smart of you. Thank you for not telling Carter and for helping me with my tests.

Thank you,

Bryan

**

Dear Bryan,

It was so sweet of you to write me that letter! You were a pleasure to have in class, and if I taught fourth grade, I would have loved to be your teacher again as well! Please know, if you ever want to stop by for a chat, my door is always open.

I have only been teaching for a few years now, but I have encountered a number of students with various learning disabilities. Your disability does not define you. Some of my brightest, most ingenuitive students have had learning disabilities (you included!). Just because it takes someone a little bit longer to complete a task does not mean the person is less intelligent, nor that the work is less substantive. Do not be ashamed of your dyslexia. It does not determine who you are as a person, nor where you will go in life. It will always be a part of you, but it does not need to define you.

I understand why you did not want your friends to know. Kids your age can be harsh when they encounter something they are unfamiliar with. But you are an amazing, sweet, and talented kid, as are your friends. If you share your world with them, give them time to adjust and understand; I have no doubt they will accept you as you are. Because dyslexia does not take away from the phenomenal human being you are constantly becoming. It just adds another wonderful hue to the rainbow that is you!

Best wishes and best of luck in your new school year,

Mrs. Crawley

You taught me what it means to trust someone

Mrs. D.,

I know flowery words are not something we typically exchange given our dynamic, the department you run, and the courses of yours that I have been in, but I want to thank you for everything you have done for me and the lessons you have taught me and how much care you have shown every student under your care.

You taught me what a healthy student-administration relationship looks like by giving me the courage to speak out on issues that troubled me – by encouraging me to continue learning outside of your classroom through articles that helped you grow or gave you joy – and by sticking by my side when I had to take action for my fellow students.

You, more than any other person at our school, made me feel like the students were cared for by giving consistent and thorough feedback that would help me not only with your class, but with classes that I took later – by pairing students with other classmates to encourage diverse thinking and growth of knowledge from both parties – and most importantly, by stepping between me and a former student whom I had broken up with when he showed up to your class to harass, scare, and threaten my well-being. You even taught me how to get through a group project without wanting to cry – a lesson I use every semester.

You put up with all my quirks as a student, my persistent need for more feedback than other students in my classes, my desire for advice on what classes to take, whether or not to pursue certain academic opportunities, and my unnecessary rambles about DC vs. Marvel in all their various forms (even my attempts to connect them to coursework to understand new concepts).

There was never a time in class where I felt like I was not allowed to ask a question, even when I fear my queries were that of a common fool – you made sure that I and any other student could ask, even adding your own experiences of being a student, to ensure we felt safe to learn.

Though we have not directly dealt with my concerns over my degree, in that I have had many points where I have lost all motivation to finish my associate's degrees, you have always found a way to make learning enjoyable in a way where I forget for a while that I am struggling to push through my courses. When a class gets rough, I think of how you would approach teaching the subject, and then, I try to teach myself that way.

There are no words for how much I wish I could convey a proper thank you for those lessons and show of care.

Thank you for being a resource that does not end when I move on to other colleges, degrees, and careers. Thank you for showing me that any subject can be fun when you approach it right. Thank you for protecting me as a student and my interests as a student. And thank you for being someone I can look up to.

I am so glad I took your classes, and I hope that I keep the lessons that you have taught me for as long as they will be of use.

Best wishes to you,

Alexis Watson-Lowe

***

Alexis,

Thank you for your thoughtful letter. You have been a pleasure to teach and I feel lucky you have been my student for more than one semester.

I always try to provide a space where my students feel comfortable speaking out on issues that trouble them, and I hope to provide an atmosphere where they can learn and grow. You are at such a pivotal point in your life, and I feel humbled to play a part in that, even through just the small things...like getting through group projects.

The bigger things are why I treasure being a teacher. Being able to provide comfort for you after your breakup or encourage you to continue classes to earn your associate's degree are bigger lessons than I could ever teach in the classroom.

I have never "put up" with your quirks; instead, I love them, and I am so pleased you are a strong, confident young woman who isn't afraid to show them. Your need for feedback tells me you care about improving yourself, wanting advice on academic opportunities tells me you value your time but also want to learn as much as you can, and your DC vs. Marvel connections were simply a joy to listen to!

It means so much to me that I am a role model to you, Alexis. But I want you to know I learn and grow from my students, each and every day. Your tenacity and grit to keep going are inspiring. I am so blessed to have been your teacher!

Best wishes,

Mrs. D.

Thank you for speaking to my heart

Dear Dr. Davis,

Talent, Tal.ent, noun. Natural aptitude or skill. Talent is a trait that many personally wish to have or wish to be acknowledged as possessing. A person could, perhaps, imagine that Kobe Bryant was told often he had basketball talent. That simple acknowledgement of basketball talent heard often could have been a reinforcement for him to use, fueling his dream or sense of self that he felt deep within. Perhaps a child will show talent in coloring and drawing. A parent's encouragement and acknowledgement of the child's talent may lead the child to a successful career as an artist later in life. These people will both bring change to the world with their talents. What many might not realize is, the simple effect of being seen with talent can have a powerful effect on a person, or the simple act of not acknowledging—or worse, saying someone does not have talent—can hold just as powerful reaction in the negative. Being seen to have talent can instill a sense of worth and drive in a person. The simple fact of knowing someone sees any talent can motivate a person to overcome challenges that they may have thought at first to be unobtainable. The possibilities of the power of acknowledgement are endless.

You saw talent in me when others in my past hadn't. Not only did you see my talent, but you shared your view of me with me. I don't think you will ever know the emesis gift you gave me by doing that. You gave it so freely and openly, and shared in detail why I was talented. The care in your delivery of why you saw me as talented became a powerful tool of motivation for me. I do not know yet if you knew, I suffer from imposter syndrome. I know you had no idea that in my past, in my first week in high school, I had a teacher tell me that I "wasn't smart enough for the International Baccalaureate program". At that point, as a teenager, I shut down. I allow myself to accept an idea someone else had about me and not my own view of me. I allow the idea that I had no talent in learning to win. That I, perhaps, should not dream big or worry about college at all.

Thankfully, that idea someone else had of me only held me back 18 years. I grew brave at first with the help of friends who share a vision like yours. Talent finding vision. Friends and a few family members who saw my talent and freely shared encouragement. I started to question myself and ask, "why not me?" Armed with wisdom, which I believe, comes from experience, life trials, and a bit of curiosity to find my talent, I enrolled in college. I listened to those who believed in me and signed up for school to overcome my fear that I was not smart.

I am thankful for that brave moment. See, that moment is how our paths crossed. It feels strange at times, that a man I have yet had the pleasure to meet in person, has empowered me so much. It also speaks to the beautiful power of acknowledgement. Today, it is in that power, that I want to say thank you. Dr. Paul Davis, thank for your acknowledgement in my talent to hold an intelligent discussion. Your comment stating that my schoolwork was as good as or better than some of your graduate students in only my second semester of college empowered me to keep sharing in my classes.

I want to thank you for acknowledging that you liked my writing style, and that it was well-supported. I never write with grammar in mind, but more to connect with the person reading my writing. I want my reader to feel as if they are right in front of me having a conversation with me. Your acknowledgement in my writing talent keeps me brave in sharing my written ideas and thoughts with others in my own personal way. You gave me the courage to keep being me. To not listen to other people's ideas of me or my writing. Thank you for your acknowledgement in my talent on seeing and hearing both sides of the argument. That I should be writing public policy papers. Thank you for telling me that I was the top student out of your classes of two hundred. That was a power moment, as I was near the bottom of my high school class of two hundred when I graduated. See that acknowledgement, in itself, might be the steppingstone of major growth for me. You see that acknowledgement helped me tear down that 18-year-old wall built by myself with the help of a teacher blind to my talents. The wall that I was not smart crumbled, and I stepped further out of my comfort zone. With your suggestion, I applied for New Leadership of Nevada. That experience of being accepted and taking in all the wisdom of the other leaders I met was invaluable. I am learning to take my leadership skills to the next level. I am overcoming my fear that I do not understand politics and government and am getting involved. Someone who just met me asked me, "So, when are you running for office? Let's get you on some boards." Your acknowledgement is helping me to bring the change in myself I crave and the trust and willingness to bring change in our community. Change deeper than I ever imagined I could possibly do. I do not know just yet what I am going to do or how as I am still currently in my own metamorphosis, but I do know it will be something, and it will help many. Thank you for teaching me the power of acknowledging talent. I look forward to the day we meet and the next time I can acknowledge someone else's talent. I just know that I'm going to bring change to the world with my talents.

With much thanks and respect,

Your former student,

Cheryl

***

Hello Cheryl,

I am absolutely humbled and honored by your fabulous letter to me. You have earned all of my praise and respect for you. I have been teaching college for almost 50 years, and every once in a great while ,I will come across someone like you, Cheryl, with an extraordinary intellectual talent. It literally brings joy to my heart to see you flourishing like you have been doing here in college.

I strongly suspect that you will achieve great success on multiple levels in your life; and will make a strong contribution to the betterment of our society.

I wish you the absolute best in your life now and in the future as well.

Sincerely,

Paul B. Davis. Ph.D.

LETTER 12

You acknowledged my talents

Dear Mrs. Anderson,

I wanted to write you a letter to thank you for making my first day of school not so bad. Most of the time when I start a new school, it's really hard. Because my dad is in the military, I have been to four schools so far, which is a lot. I'm used to being the new kid, but I'm not used to having a good first day.

Thank you for treating me normally, even though I use a wheelchair. I know you were probably wondering what was wrong with me, but thank you for not asking. Since you are probably still curious, I'll tell you: I was born this way. I have never walked, but my brain is okay. That's what my mom says anyway. Most of the time, though, people act like my brain is not okay, and they will not want to talk to me, which makes me sad.

There were some not-so-nice kids today. One of the kids said I don't belong in your class. They were being really mean to me. One of them wanted to wheel me around even when I said "no!" When they tried to do it anyway, I felt alone and sort of helpless. I could not walk away, even though that is what lots of grown-ups say to do when other kids are mean.

But guess what? Those meanies were not even in our class! And when you saw them treating me badly, you sent them to the principal's office right away. They even tried to get away with it by just saying "sorry", but you stood up for me. That made me feel really happy and sparkly inside.

I have never had a teacher that was in a wheelchair, like me. I think that when I grow up, I want to be a teacher like you. Because you were able to help me feel like I was a normal kid and that I could have a normal job when I was a grown up.

Thank you for being there for me, even though I was the new kid.

Love,

Selena, age nine

***

Dear Selena,

Thank you for your kind note. It means a lot to me to hear that I was helpful in making sure you had a good first day! It's never easy being the new kid. I didn't move around as much as you have, but I did move when I was in seventh grade. It was hard, but I met some really great friends and had some teachers who inspired me to become a teacher, as well!

I was not wondering what was "wrong with you" because I didn't see anything wrong in the first place, although it warms my heart that you feel comfortable enough to share with me. I only saw a beautiful, smart young lady who I was lucky enough to have in my class. I first started using my wheelchair in high school after I got in a skiing accident. I know people are not always kind about people who may look different than them or use different things to get around or help their bodies. I was bullied a great deal during my senior year of high school (my last year of school), which made me feel like I shouldn't even try to go to college.

But I had a teacher who told me not to give up! So, I went to college to become a teacher. I'm really glad I did, because while I was in college, I met some of my best friends and even my husband. I know you're still young and not even thinking about getting married, but my point is that even though there are "meanies" out there, there are good people as well.

I never want you to feel helpless or like you can't succeed. You can always come to me if you have a problem or question...or if you feel like you are being treated unfairly. Even if you have to move again, I will be your pen pal.

Sending love back,

Mrs. A.

You opened my mind

Good afternoon Mr. D.,

It has been a year-and-a-half since we last spoke, and six years since being in 8th grade, in your Honors Algebra 1 class. To this day, you are the number one teacher who has made a huge impact on my life, even years later, I remember that poem you gave us one day in class, and I still have it laminated on my desk.

It resonated with me then, when I was just 14 struggling with math. Since then, I've graduated with my associate's degree six days before graduating high school, become Chief Medical Scribe at my job, and am currently tackling genetics, physics, and organic chemistry. Through the years I've struggled at times in classes, but I've always remembered the words of the poem you gave all of your students called "Our Deepest Fears" by Marianne Williamson, that I continue to keep in my desk on days where I fall back into my thoughts of doubt. "Our deepest fear is not that we are inadequate. Our deepest fear is that we are powerful beyond measure. It is our light, not our darkness that most frightens us. Your playing small does not serve the world. There is nothing enlightened about shrinking so that other people won't feel insecure around you. We are all meant to shine, as children do. It's not just in some of us; it's in everyone. And as we are liberated from our own fear, our presence automatically liberates others."

Despite still having to face some of my deepest fears, I have been able to continue to face more and more of them as time goes on, remembering your encouragement and belief in me, when I doubted myself daily. You showed me I can achieve more than I originally think, always. Thank you for being the most effective teacher at leaving an important, lasting impression on me, that has continued to push me to my greatest potential, even now.

Sincerely,

Kaitlyn

***

Hi Kaitlyn,

Even though it has been awhile, I have not forgotten your sweet smile and determined attitude. It is so good to hear from you! I am amazed at your accomplishments, although not surprised. You have always been a driven student and to know that I, and that poem, played a small part in that is humbling.

I know math is not everyone's strong suit. There were times growing up that I, too, struggled with the subject. When I first read "Our Deepest Fears", I knew I wanted to use it as I began teaching, even though I am not a literary teacher. I am so grateful it had the same profound impact on you that it did on me. I have always wondered if using poetry in math class seems silly, so it means a lot to me that you reached out to tell me how much it meant to you.

Never doubt yourself, Kaitlyn. You have the ability to do whatever you want. I know that I am far from the only person who sees this in you. Graduating college before high school is a prime example of this.

Thank you for letting me know that you have conquered your fears and made it through even more challenging math classes! I really enjoyed hearing from you.

-Mr. D.

You helped me find my voice

Dear Sensei Dawn,

It seems a little strange to write to you out of the blue, but I wanted to thank you for a lot of things. Mainly for helping me become the person I am today.

I started karate with my brother when I was only nine years old. I was shy, quiet, practically invisible little girl, and I preferred reading over making loud noises and punching anyone. But when I stepped into your dojo, the first thing I had to learn was how to use my voice. To say "stop" when someone was in my space and I didn't like it, and to say "go away and leave me alone," when they didn't listen the first time. I learned to punch, and I learned to kick. I learned kata and how to fight against four people at once.

Your other senseis would give us drills to make our punches and kicks stronger and faster, to make *us* stronger and faster. We were drilled on all twelve katas, the Takeukes, and the Haiyans, until we had memorized every step as one beautiful, deadly dance. I stood in the middle, hemmed in by four students, and punched and kicked at the bags they used to trap me. At first, I could only punch and kick for a few seconds. But as I got stronger, as my stamina improved, I got better. I was able to last longer and longer within the ring, until finally, I was able to punch and kick my way out.

I learned I could do fifty push-ups and crunches by the time I was ten. I learned I could do a flying side-kick that could knock a grown-man over on his back. But most of all, I learned that with hard work and discipline, I could achieve and gain anything I wanted to.

I went to classes for five years in your dojo. I sweated, I practiced, I tried my best every single time. And at the end of it, I didn't just gain a black belt. I gained the knowledge that I had my own voice, that could be loud when I needed it to be, and quiet when I wanted it to be. I learned I was strong enough to protect myself, but I had the control to only use my power when absolutely necessary. And when I tied that black belt around my waist, I *knew* that I could succeed at whatever I set my mind to accomplish, so long as I had the patience, the dedication, and the discipline to follow it through.

I learned a lot in your dojo, Sensei. But I think the most important lesson was the one you taught me. If anyone looked at you, they would've seen a slight, blonde woman with blue eyes. But you were more than that. You were a single mom, raising two children, and hating the jobs you took to pay the bills. You managed to get your blackbelt, to start up your own successful business—one that has educated and enriched the lives of children for twenty-five years—and make your mark as an educator, a businesswoman, and an inspiration. You managed to do so much without any help, just the dedication to your vision, the determination to see it through, and the willpower to keep going, no matter how tired you were at the end of every day.

Two years ago, you hired me to be a sensei in your dojo. I was given the job to train, to mold the minds of the young minds who looked to me as a role model, and to enrich their lives and teach them life lessons to carry with them as they got older. It was the highest honor you could bestow.

Every day when I put on my *gei*, and tied my belt, I was reminded once again of the privilege I had been given, and I was thankful. Every time I stepped on to the mat, it was always with the intention to do my best job, but also to inspire my students the same way you inspired me.

Right now, things are difficult, and it pains me every day that the dojos are closed and I can't see the kids every day like I used to. But when they reopen once more, I'll be there, ready to do my job as a teacher, ready to teach them everything you taught me, once more.

Sincerely,

Sensei Ruby

***

Dear Sensei Ruby,

Thank you for your beautiful letter. It warmed my heart to know how much you enjoyed your lessons and my teachings. I remember watching you grow during your classes, and I was always proud of every little milestone you achieved. I am so proud that you have become such a confident and incredible young woman.

(You know of course) I began karate as a young adult because I wanted to feel stronger in this scary world. I was very shy (like you), and I really didn't know how to stand up for myself. I was also drawn to the philosophy of martial arts; the idea that you can control your mind, body, and spirit was very intriguing. I liked the mystery of it. I thought if I could understand that philosophy and bring together the power of this, then surely, anything would be possible. And I was right!

I signed up for lessons, but they only had two classes per week, and I wanted to do karate every single day. So, I went home after each class and practiced in the mirror. I practiced every single move we had learned and did it 100 times on each side until I felt I understood it. That is how I got good. I set my own schedule, I worked hard, and I made sure I showed up for practice whether I was at the dojo or at home. This life skill is very powerful. You can use it for everything you want to achieve in your career. Show up, do the work, repeat, repeat, repeat. This kind of discipline will make you a success at whatever you choose to do; work, relationships, health, fitness, creativity, whatever it is you put your mind to. So, go forth and conquer your dreams by using this powerful life skill of discipline in mind, body, and spirit!

I am honored that you think so much of me and my journey. It took a lot of hard work and dedication, just like earning your blackbelt! I never dreamed my little dojo would become five over the years, but ultimately, it was never about how many I had. It was about all the wonderfully special and amazing children within (like you and your brother) who made my life and my work so worthwhile. It made me so happy to see you rise up and become a teacher and change the lives of your students. And while I would love to see you in the dojo again, I know that no matter what you chose to do in the future, you will succeed.

Sincerely,

Sensei Dawn

I loved you for listening to me

Dear Mrs. McMillan,

You have been such an amazing teacher and friend. I learned so much about what it means to be a good person in your class and how to stand up for myself.

Your morning meditations always made me really happy and relaxed. It was so nice to hear those words so early in the morning. The slow breathing always made me sleepy, but it was a good sleepy. One time, I was so relaxed I fell asleep in class, but only for a minute! I know not everyone liked the meditations at first. A couple kids, including Michael, would talk through them or get up from their desks and walk around. You were so patient, I couldn't believe it. You never got mad. You just kept that same soft voice and nicely asked them to sit down and be quiet. I think even Michael liked them by the end of school. He actually sat and listened to what you were saying. They really helped me. I hope they helped him, too.

Thank you for letting me talk to you after class when I did not understand something, or if someone had said something mean. I didn't want people to hear my stutter in class, so I didn't want to ask too many questions. I think another reason I liked the morning meditations is because my stutter wasn't so bad when they were over.

A lot of times, other kids would say mean things or make fun of how I talk when you were not looking. I had a hard time defending myself, because I couldn't get the words out right, and I did not want to look stupid. You told me I could come to you any time someone was mean, and you would help me. That happened a lot. I remember one time, Michael took my Ninja Turtle book away because he said

I couldn't read. He didn't think I could read because I stutter. I tried to tell him to give it back, but I was really upset, and I couldn't say it. I hit him and got in trouble with Ms. Shay, because Michael told on me. He lied and said I tried to take his book, even though it is mine. She believed him, because I was only crying and couldn't say that it was my book. Ms. Shay made me stay inside for recess. When I told you about it at lunch, you told me it wasn't my fault. You called Michael in and made him give the book back and took away his recess for a week. That was the only time I have ever seen you get angry. I was a little scared, but also happy that you did that. Michael stopped bothering me for a long time, and I got my book back. You said that hitting is wrong, but defending yourself is good. Thank you for helping me defend myself. I promise I won't hit anybody ever again.

Thank you for always helping me and standing up to bullies for me. I don't cry anymore when people are mean to me, because I know that they are wrong for doing that. I still want my stutter to get better, so I can tell people not to be mean, but I am so happy that you are around to help me.

Thank you,

Will

***

Dear Will,

Anytime you need help, Will, you just let me know! You were a fantastic student, and I'm so glad I had you in my class. It is so important to stand up for yourself and for others when they can't do it themselves. If you keep working on it, I have no doubt that you will be able to conquer your stutter and tell bullies off for yourself. In the meantime, you should never hesitate to reach out to a teacher, parent, or other grownup if someone is bullying you or anyone around you. Bullying is never acceptable; you never need to tolerate it. We need to speak up whenever we see injustice in the world. You never know who could be hurting in silence.

You are a very intelligent little boy with a big heart, and I know that you are going to do great things when you grow up. You have a deeper understanding of injustice and cruelty than most children your age do. I know it is painful now. Hopefully, you will be able to use your experiences to better understand the struggles of others. Let any ill will sent your way be converted into compassion. That is true strength. But, at the same time, make sure you never let any of the bullies put you down or keep you down. You have deep, inherent worth that some people may never understand, but will never be able to take away from you.

Thank you for letting me know how I have impacted your life. It truly means a lot to me.

Mrs. McMillan

Thank you for helping me explore

Dear Dr. Hargis,

I hope this letter finds you well. I wanted to thank you for how much you have helped me spread my wings and fly in Phi Theta Kappa, as well as specifically within our chapter, Alpha Mu Tau. Your wisdom and consistent encouragement to step out of my comfort zone has allowed me to do things I never would have done before, due to nerves that naturally come when you are stepping out of your comfort zone. Whether that may be holding the title of three different leadership positions within our chapter, singing the national anthem for the Texas Honors Institute, or leading the Service committee to a successful Project MeWe campaign, you have been here for me throughout all of it, encouraging me to take leaps and bounds and growing as a leader and a scholar. Before being part of Phi Theta Kappa and part of the amazing chapter that is Alpha Mu Tau, I let myself listen to the negative voice inside my head, and miss out on opportunities. The reason I say this is to not create a pity party, but, rather, to show you one of the many ways you impacted my life. Throughout my time in Alpha Mu Tau, you have encouraged me to try new things, and from trying, I will learn so many new things about myself that were hidden under the surface, of what I am able to accomplish when I believe in myself and in the endless possibilities ahead of me. The funny thing is, when I became the Chair of Service,

I never expected that I would be here leading Project MeWe, and partnering with the Counseling Department at Collin College to help guide the project to be as successful as it can be. To be honest, I didn't know what I expected, but that is what made it enjoyable, as I was along for the ride on where this year took me. And I have to tell you, it's already been a great one. That is one of the many ways you are awesome, as you just know these kinds of things, more specifically, what member will excel in what officer/chair position, and help make our chapter shine. I don't know how you do it! You must have a crystal ball or something haha! Overall, I am so thankful for you being one of my biggest supporters throughout all of this. I truly couldn't have done any of this without you and the rest of our amazing chapter by my side rooting me on. I know for sure that even after I leave Collin, and I venture off into the big wide world, all of these memories, and more, I will take with me and will forever be thankful for being part of Alpha Mu Tau. Love you, Dr. Hargis!

Sincerely,

Alexis Merker

***

Alexis,

You are the embodiment of PTK for so many reasons, the least of which is you are present at all Chapter events, programs, and meetings, and personally contribute to all projects...basically, you get involved!

After what I believe was a big gulp of the PTK Kool-Aid, you quickly understood the magnitude and breadth of opportunities available through Phi Theta Kappa, and have been instrumental in questioning the status quo to ensure Chapter growth and development. With a focus on what will benefit the Chapter, help the officer team, and advantage our members, you see the true benefit to living the hallmarks of Phi Theta Kappa.

What I have come to realize is that you are intensely fair, committed to moral and intellectual honesty, and espouse a high ethical standard in all actions. Though young, I have never seen you absently texting or surfing the net. When people are with you, we immediately notice that you are truly present in every endeavor.

All of this would be wonderful on its own, but it is coupled with a consistently positive attitude and an ability to actively listen with the end goal being what is best for the **Chapter,** rather than any *one* individual. Then, you take the lessons and grow to help with your next endeavor!

I have enjoyed getting to know you and hope that we can remain in contact, so that I can be a part of celebrating the successful person you are sure to become!

Thank you,

Jessica Hargis, Ph.D.

LETTER 17

Thank you for teaching me to dance

Dear Mrs. L,

I'm not sure if you remember me, but this is Taylor. I took your PE class a couple years ago, when I was in middle school. Most kids didn't like your class (actually, I didn't like it most of the time, either), but there was one unit I loved: dance.

You taught us all sorts of dances, and no one sat out. We did hip hop and jazz and ballroom dancing...and we did ballet. I first saw dancers do ballet when my mom took me and my sister to see *The Nutcracker* for Christmas one year. It was so cool. The dancers looked like they were flying. They were so limber and flexible, and the costumes were amazing. They told a whole story without words. I didn't think that would be possible, but it is!

Ever since I saw *The Nutcracker*, I wanted to learn ballet, but my dad always said no. He said that boys shouldn't dance ballet because it's too girly. When I told my friends I wanted to learn, they thought I was joking. So, I pretended I was joking, so they wouldn't make fun of me. But secretly, I still wanted to learn. I wanted to do those cool jumps and stuff that I saw all the dancers do in *The Nutcracker*. Sometimes, when no one was home, I would look up videos on my laptop and try and teach myself. But I always got hurt and had to pretend I fell down while riding my bike or something.

But then, we did the dancing unit in your class. A bunch of boys were complaining and said dancing was for girls. I'm sorry I joined them; I just didn't want them to make fun of me afterwards. It meant a lot to me when you corrected them and said dancing is for anyone. When you showed a super cool video of *The Nutcracker*

and pointed out the boy dancers, it made my heart really happy! I felt like I could finally learn how to dance, and no one would make fun of me.

No one did make fun of me during our dance unit, since everyone was doing it, but I decided I wanted to continue lessons beyond that. I told my dad that dancers could be boys, and I saved up my own money to pay for lessons. I also showed him the same video you showed us in class. He thought it was cool I was standing up for what I really wanted to do, and he said it was okay if I wanted to dance. But my "friends" found out, and they made fun of me anyway, even after you said boys can dance, too.

But guess what? When they made fun of me this time, it didn't bother me. Because I remembered you telling them that dancing isn't just a "girly" thing and that it's good exercise. I also really like dancing and I have super-cool friends there. So, I didn't really care what they thought anymore.

Thank you for teaching me that I can go after my dreams, even if other people tell me no. I probably never would have danced if it wasn't for you. And guess what? Next week, I'm dancing in *The Nutcracker*!

Sincerely,

Taylor

Dear Taylor,

As a PE teacher, I know not everyone is a fan of running a mile or playing dodgeball. That's why I try to do some different things in my class—like dancing—and it is incredible to hear how much this unit impacted you.

As a little girl, I ran into similar problems. I always wanted to do "tomboy" things, like baseball and football. I also enjoyed playing in the mud, much to my mother's dismay. It was a daily challenge to get me into anything other than a t-shirt and jeans! Wearing a dress was out of the picture completely.

The point is, I understand your struggles, which is, perhaps, why I chose "dance" as a unit in the first place. I don't think gender stereotypes have a place in our society anymore. I want to show kids that girls can do anything boys can do and vice versa.

There will always be people in this world who don't understand our dreams and goals. I am so proud of you for going after your dreams of being a dancer, in spite of a few kids' opinions. The fact that the video I showed in class was able to convince your father is amazing, and I am so happy for you. Thank you very much for sharing.

I would love to come watch you dance next week! *The Nutcracker* has always been one of my favorite ballets, and it will forever hold a special meaning, now that I know of your connection to it!

Keep breaking down barriers!

Love,

Mrs. L.

Thank you for showing me life is a journey

Dear Mrs. P.,

I wanted to write you a letter to thank you for believing in me and acknowledging my talents. I was really nervous about taking your class this year, because I was going to be the only 8th grader in a class full of 9th graders - high schoolers! But you told me that my writing was amazing and that I needed to be in your class. This made me feel really special.

Thank you for realizing what I needed to grow as a writer. I was feeling really bored in 8th grade English, and I have learned so much in your class. You have done a lot of really cool projects that we didn't do when I was in middle school. My favorite was when we did a project that focused on all the important people in our lives. I loved being able to celebrate all the important people to me, and you even helped me make a cool video to bring it all together. I always thought English class was just about writing papers, but your class showed me it can be about a lot of things.

I also got to expand my vocabulary a lot this year through the "donut wars" competition! I was so excited when our class won! I learned a lot of really amazing words and got to eat some yummy donuts (during class!) because of it. Thank you for making learning so fun...and tasty!

I was really sad when you told me today that you are leaving to go teach at a school that is closer to your house. I wish you would stay at our school, because I think you are an awesome teacher, and I wish I could take more of your classes. But I understand that you need to be closer to your home. If I was an adult, I'd probably want to be closer to my home, too.

Thank you for making my first high school class so fun. When I am a 9th grader for real this fall, I am not going to be nervous now. I am going to be excited!

Sincerely,

Liza

***

Dear Liza,

Thank you for your letter! I'm so glad you had fun in my class this semester. I know the difference between eighth and ninth grade seems pretty big to you, but it really isn't. In fact, once you get to college, you'll probably take classes with people who are five or even ten years older than you - isn't that crazy?

You are such a talented writer. When your eighth grade teacher showed me some of your work, I knew you had to be in my class. I hope you never stop writing, and I hope skipping a grade will help you to be able to advance your talents sooner.

I never wanted my class to be about "boring" essays, so I am so glad you enjoyed our projects, videos, and donut wars with the other ninth grade class! Expanding your vocabulary is a must, especially since you will take the SAT in a couple years, and I am so excited we could do it in a fun way! I would never be **lackadaisical** about teaching you vocabulary words. ;)

It breaks my heart to leave my students, and it was a difficult call to make. But my own daughters are getting older, and I want to be home for important things like prom and science fairs! I know it would make you sad if your mom couldn't be there for you during high school, right? But don't worry - I want to stay in touch with all you awesome students. Please keep in touch with me and tell me about the awesome adventures you are having and any great writing you have been doing!

You are a star, Liza, and I am so proud of you!

~Mrs. P.

Thank you for being my sunshine

Dear Ms. Leeanna,

I miss you so much! Thank you for being one of my favorite teachers ever! You're beautiful and kind, and I love how fun you are! You always have a way of cheering me up on a bad day! There's never a moment where we're not laughing or smiling. I love how you always have a big smile on your face. You're my sunshine on a rainy day! We look like twins because of our freckles, hair, eyes, and our names. When I grow up, I want to be just like you because you do very well in school and you're a great role model.

Love,

Leena Spiller

xoxo

Dear Leena,

I miss you! I hope you are doing well! I wanted to say thank you for being one of the first and best kids I've ever worked with.

You were always one of the sweetest, and most mature girls. I always say how much you remind me of myself, with the hair, freckles, and even our names!! Your personality and maturity also resembles me from when I was your age. Keep doing everything you are doing, and you are going to grow up to be so successful!! No matter what kind of day I was having, I always looked forward to hanging out with you when you would come off the aftercare bus. It was refreshing to have a student so well-behaved and courteous, after a stressful day of teaching pre-k! The other kids looked up to you, too. You are a role model to them all. I'm so proud of you for going to a new school this year, moving to a new house, and being in school virtually all at the same time. I know it must have been hard to adjust, but I know you're doing amazing now. Just know I am *so* proud of you always, and I'm thankful I got to have you in one of my first groups of kids I ever worked with.

Love and miss you! Give your new puppy, Penny, a kiss from me!!

Keep being awesome. Xoxo.

Miss Leeanna

Thank you for making me laugh

Dear Mrs. Tee,

You are my favorite teacher. I know I have told you that before, but since you usually smile and nod in the way that makes me think you don't *really* believe me, I thought I would write you a letter to tell you why.

I am not very good at math and science. When I learned that every ninth grader had to take "Intro to Physics", I was really nervous because I looked up what "physics" was, and it was basically math and science smashed together into one course.

One of my friends is in tenth grade, and she doesn't like math and science either. I asked her about intro to physics, and she said that she didn't want to take it at first, but you were such a fun teacher you made it alright...fun, even! I decided to give it a shot, even though I was still skeptical.

On the first day of class, I had so much fun I didn't want to leave! The scavenger hunt you set up around the science lab was a blast, and I still learned a lot about lab safety. As the semester went on, you taught us a lot about physics while making it fun. You even did one-on-one tutoring with me when I needed help. You changed the wording of the problems to keep it interesting - we even did problems where we sent our pets to the moon!

One day when it snowed outside, we did an impromptu snowball fight and calculated the velocity and density of the snowballs. I had never had a teacher who was willing to cancel class for a snowball fight, only to weave in learning in a fun way! I will never forget that day.

You are truly the most incredible teacher ever. Thanks to you, I made a 97 percent in a class that is basically my two worst subjects combined. You have given me the confidence that I can succeed in any subject I want!

With gratitude,

Rachelle

***

Dear Rachelle,

Your letter made my day! You are right - I have many students who say I'm their favorite teacher, but we have so many incredible teachers here that I know they likely have more than one favorite teacher.

I know most students are nervous about taking physics, which is actually why I love teaching it! Taking a "scary" subject and making it fun is so rewarding. It also helps build confidence early on in high school. Now, you don't have to be afraid of your other math and science classes!

Sending our pets to the moon is a much more fun way to do physics than just calculating a ball being thrown, don't you think? Making learning fun is key, because you will retain the information better! Always remember this. When you have a hard problem, don't hesitate to swap out the information for things that do interest you. It really does help! The same goes for the snowball fight. I knew with the fresh snow on the ground, you all wouldn't learn anything anyway. So why not have some fun...and learn at the same time??

I'm so glad you had a fun year in my class. I hope to see you next year in Earth Science!

~Mrs. Tee

LETTER 21

Thank you for helping me explore

Dear Mr. W.,

Wow...where do I begin? It's actually hard to believe I am graduating. It felt like this day would never get here, but it arrived in a flash.

From the moment we met at high school orientation, I knew I was in for a ride. Your quirky spirit and fun outlook on life was contagious. When I learned you were heading up the student council, I was really excited. It was one of the first clubs I signed up for. You never made me feel like my ideas were dumb or wrong, but actually gave me a voice and confidence. We were able to put on some really great fundraisers, dances, and harvest festivals, weren't we? As I got older, I assumed officer positions, with a little prodding from you, and I am so grateful that I did. I have grown so much, and I can't wait to find another group in college to get involved with. But I'll always remember the student council was where I started!

Your teaching style was unique, and when I took my first class with you, I was really surprised (in a good way!). You didn't give tests, but challenged our knowledge through a "game show" format. I learned so much about astronomy from you, and I will never forget our "star gazing" night, when we all stayed late to star gaze together, and you made the whole class hot chocolate to stay warm and toasty!

But the thing I remember most about you is that you never stopped asking me questions. Throughout most of my school career, I was used to asking the teachers questions and them telling me answers. But before you, no one had bothered to ask me what I thought, to ask me questions. It was different; it made me feel as though my voice actually mattered.

When I became a senior, I was too busy to be as involved with the student council as much as I had been. Even so, your questions didn't stop—instead, they simply changed. You asked me questions like, "are you doing okay?" and "do you need help with anything?" You asked me if I was excited to graduate, if I got my applications in on time, and if I was taking care of myself during all this craziness.

Of course, you didn't know this, but I was a foster kid. So, my senior year was more stressful than most. I was about to turn 18 and age out of the system. I didn't know what I was going to do. No one ever really cared about me. My foster parents were rarely around, and when they were, they would never ask me how I was, nor what my plans were.

It was because of you that I stayed in high school. It was because of your questions that I felt heard. And it was because of student council that I knew I could be more than that shy girl in the back of the classroom. I decided to go to college. I know it will be hard, but I'm determined not to be a statistic.

I might be the only senior here today without proud parents in the crowd. That's okay, though. For the first time ever, I don't feel sad. Because I was able to catch your eye in the crowd and when you smiled and winked at me, it made me feel as though at least one person believed in me.

And that's all that matters.

Love,

Raya

Raya,

Your letter has blown me away. You have always struck me as a smart, witty, and mature girl, but I had no idea you were going through so much.

You are such a natural student council leader, and I was so excited when you signed up for my astronomy elective! The hot chocolate was a spur of the moment idea, but I'm glad you enjoyed it. Looking at the stars has always helped calm me and made me realize how beautiful and magical this world is. I hope it had the same effect on you.

Thank you for being such a bright spot for me these past four years. It has been a privilege to watch you grow and explore, and most importantly, come out of your shell. I can only imagine how hard life must have been growing up as a foster child. Please know, that should you ever need a "stand in" parent, I'll be there for you. And when you cross the stage at your college graduation, I will be there - cheering, crying, and with a bouquet of "congratulations" flowers.

With love,

Mr. W.

LETTER 22

Thank you for asking me questions

Dear Ms. Harlow,

I want to thank you for helping me figure out what I want to do with my life. I know I have time to think about it still, but I'm pretty sure I've got it. More sure about this than I am about anything else in my life. I'm glad that I'll be going through my last two years of high school knowing what I want my career to be. I think that will be particularly helpful as I pick out honors/AP classes, clubs/ extracurriculars, and begin looking at colleges this spring. Up until your honors English class, I had no clue what I wanted to do with my life. I feel like I came up with a different career path every day. I felt lost and anxious, and it seemed like everyone around me had a plan for "what comes next".

But in your class, I always felt calm and relaxed. I felt like I had control. Whether we were discussing a new chapter or reviewing an essay or discussing grammar, I always felt like I had a seat at the table. That my opinion mattered. That you cared about what I thought. Even when I got something wrong or we disagreed on something, you made it clear that you wanted to know more about my perspective and why I thought what I thought. From what I can tell, you did that with all of your students. That is probably why everyone wants you to be their English teacher.

No other teacher I have had here treats their students like that. They teach, and we ask questions. In your class, you asked questions of us. REAL questions about what we thought, not just the mindless prepared questions that come in the teacher lesson book. You encouraged us to examine ourselves and use our own minds, not just accept what the world tells us we should think of something. It was really difficult to adjust to at first. I am used to memorizing study guides and flashcards and diagrams, not forming my own views on the material that we cover. And then, of course, forgetting it all once the class is over. I can honestly say that your English class is the only one I've ever been in where I actually read all the books on the syllabus *and* remembered important themes, quotes, characters, related history, symbolism, and different interpretations of the text.

You made a point to not tell us how to think, but to instead encourage us to think for ourselves. You made learning fun by making us a part of it. The impact you have had on my classmates and me cannot be overstated. I do not know of a single student who did not enjoy your class. Regardless of academic ability, class rank/GPA, interest in the subject matter, personal problems, etc., students flocked to you, because you made them feel heard. You made them feel competent. You made them understand that their voice matters, too. Even at my most anxious and lost, I knew I would feel better once I stepped into your classroom. I knew you would ask all the right questions, and I would find renewed faith in my ability to come up with answers.

I am still unsure about a lot of things, but I know I am going to enjoy being a teacher.

Thank you,

Jason

Dear Jason,

This was a humbling letter to read and appreciated more than you could possibly know. Teachers have been having just as hard a time adjusting to this new normal as students, and it has been hard to stay positive. Your letter is so encouraging. My students are so important to me, and I can't stand feeling like I am not as there for them as I would like to be. I am so, so happy that I was able to help you find your purpose. You were always full of insightful questions yourself. Now, a generation of kids will benefit from your desire to help them learn and grow.

Teaching is a wonderful, fulfilling profession, but it can also be incredibly draining. It sounds like you have the perfect mindset for this job, but I must warn you that not everyone thinks the way you do. There is a lot of pressure to "teach to the test" and to focus on grades as the sole mark of success. You and I both know that there are lessons to be learned in school that could never be measured by the results of a scantron sheet. So long as you carry that with you through the rest of your schooling and your future career, you should be just fine.

Thank you so much for taking the time to write to me. I am so pleased to hear that you and your classmates remember me fondly and found some value in my class. Questioning students with the goal of making them think (not memorize) is, in my opinion, a vital part of education that is far too often overlooked. Thank you for carrying this notion on into your classroom.

Hope all is well, and that you are enjoying junior year!

Ms. Harlow

You saved my life

Dr. Warner,

You didn't know this at the time, but you changed my life. I often felt restless, like I needed to be somewhere bigger than I was. Someone more than what I was. I was exhausted with the current state of the United States (and that hasn't gotten any better, tbh). I often dreamt of running away, of being under the same stars, but a completely different view. I first wanted to study abroad as an escape. As I got older, I've realized my worldview was limited by what I'd been exposed to, which in retrospect, wasn't much. I didn't know what I wanted to be when I "grew up", but I knew it was imperative to me to expand my mind as much as possible. Meeting you was one of my first steps on a journey that would change my life.

I first said I wanted to go to India when I was 12 years old. I recently found a journal I started my senior year of high school. One of the prompts was about travel, and guess what? I said India again. I didn't realize how much of a recurring theme India was in my life.

A few months before our initial meeting, I lost my dad. My path shifted, but that shift pointed me in your direction. I was on a new journey, walking alone. I didn't know I needed a guide, but I feel like you did. You took an interest in me that no one else had before. You saw something in myself that I had never seen.

As our physical journey took us 7,970 miles across the world, but, in my estimation, brought us together. You were my teacher, my leader, and my friend. You offered me moral support when I didn't think I could ride the elephant, you offered me emotional support when people were unjustly cruel to me, you stayed by my side when I wasn't able to go down into the step well, and never once made me feel bad about it. You were there for me and showed me that on this journey, love shows up. You always show up.

When my school plans got derailed, you were there to tell me it was okay and helped me create a new plan. My journey shifted again, and you were right there. You led me when I needed you to and knew when to follow and let me carve out my own path. As my boss and my mentor, you allowed me to plan the route sometimes, so I could feel ownership on this leg of our journey.

I hope and pray that as we continue on this path of life, you will always be there, leading and following as needed. I have a feeling that we will never be far apart.

Thank you for being my guide. Thank you for being my friend. Thank you for showing me how important it is to journey and for reminding me I never have to journey alone.

Love,

Amiee Sadler

You were my life guide

Dear Coach Johnson,

Thank you for being such an amazing coach. I realize this is kind of out of the blue, but I wanted you to know how much we appreciate you. You are so supportive and work just as hard as your players do. You're always one of the first people in the gym, rain or shine, morning or night, regardless of whatever else is going on. You've made it clear that this team is important to you, and I think that makes it mean all the more to all the girls. The energy and passion you bring to every practice and game ups the already pretty intense enthusiasm we all have for this sport we love. We are so, so lucky to have you as our coach.

I was really unsure about trying out for the volleyball team in junior high, especially since we were going to be trying out with the high schoolers. But from the second we walked in the gym, you treated all of the junior high kids like we were just as important as the high schoolers. All of your older girls made us feel welcome. They showed us how to do the drills and told us how you liked to run your tryouts and practices. They were so well-trained you hardly had to lift a finger for the first half of tryouts.

I couldn't believe I made varsity as an eighth grader. I still can't believe it, even though I've been on varsity for three years now. I know I was super-nervous to be there as an eighth grader, but you made it clear to me, time and time again, that you valued hard work and talent as much as seniority. Thank you for being so patient with me and for addressing my fears that I didn't belong on the team. The one game I got to start as an eighth grader is one of my favorite memories. It made me feel like I could do anything, so long as I put the work in.

You have taught me that focus, hard work, and positivity are crucial to a successful team environment. I have seen (and I know you have, too) some truly miserable teams with coaches who get down and out over the smallest mistakes. Their bad attitude throws off the whole team. It's like they don't trust their players to recover from mistakes. We know you have faith in us, even when we make mistakes. You never hesitate to correct us, but you always make us feel like we'll get it the next time around. "Focus on the next play;" I've heard you yell that from the sidelines more times than I can count. You've taught us that dwelling on our mistakes, instead of focusing on how we will improve, can only lead to disaster. I think that attitude is a huge part of why we are so successful as a team.

You also taught me a lot about time management. Working around three-hour practices forced me to really pay attention to my schedule, so that I would have enough time for homework and other extracurriculars. You had a plan for every practice. You knew what drills you wanted to run, what tapes you wanted to watch, and how long each segment of practice would last, right down to the second. I think I learned a lot from watching you manage the practice schedule, and I incorporated that into my own scheduling.

What sets you apart from other coaches, at least in my book, is how much effort you put into fostering a healthy team environment. We are never pitted against each other. It is never about the individual.

There are no superstars in your eyes. We are a team, through and through. I know *so* many prima donna stars on other teams at our school. Funnily enough, none of their teams are nearly as successful as ours...

Thank you for showing up every day for our team, for being endlessly supportive, and for choosing to pass your knowledge and love of the game on to us. Volleyball has been the best part of my high school experience, and you are a large part of the reason why.

Thank you so much,

Maggie

***

Dear Maggie,

You girls are so important to me. I received your letter this morning and read it during breakfast. My husband had to ask me why I was crying into my eggs. Thank you so much for this wonderful, heartfelt letter. I am so happy to hear that I have been able to enrich your lives. Volleyball has always been a passion of mine, and I have spent a significant portion of my adult life trying to pass that passion on. I can't tell you how nice it is to know I have had some success!

One of the reasons I love volleyball so much is because it is a pure team sport. Basketball, soccer, hockey, etc. all present the opportunity for a 'prima donna' personality to take over. In volleyball, there really cannot be a "star". You are fully reliant on your teammates, and they are reliant on you. If there is any drama, any weak link in the chain, the whole team goes down. You win together, and you lose together.

I have always loved the unifying effect volleyball can have on a group of people. We are all so much more powerful as a united front, both on and off the court.

You are completely right; positivity, focus, and hard work are crucial to making a team operate successfully. I have made those ideas pillars of every facet of my life, and they have always served me well. If you know what you want, are willing to work as hard as you can to get it, and won't let mistakes or naysayers slow you down (just "focus on the next play", instead), I know you will accomplish amazing things in your life.

You are a talented player and an all-around wonderful person. You have embraced hard work, positivity, and focus wholeheartedly, and I have seen how your enthusiasm encourages your teammates. Your teammates look up to you for good reason. I am so thrilled that I get to coach you for these next two years and watch you continue to grow as a player and a person.

Thank you,

Coach J.

You taught me how to work with others

Dear Ms. Thompson,

Thank you for saving my life, literally. I am almost certain I would have died, had you not been on the field trip to the aquarium. It was my own fault, really. I should know better by now than to eat food from someone else's parent, even if they're SUPER, SUPER SURE it doesn't have any tree nuts in it (I'm looking at you, Tiffany's mom…).

I guess no one else on the field trip had ever seen someone have an allergic reaction before. Well, I know Simon has, because we've been friends since the second grade, but he had gone off with Jenny and… I probably shouldn't talk about that. Anyways, when I was flopping around on the floor like one of the many slippery creatures in the tanks would have done, the whole class, parents and teachers included, could only huddle around me, gasp, and stare. I think Mrs. La Fountaine thought I was choking, because I vaguely remember her smacking me on the back. Someone should tell her she's not allowed to hit kids anymore; this is the twenty-first century after all.

Thank god you remembered that I need to carry an EpiPen at all times. I saw you take it out of my backpack and stick it in my leg like a total pro. I get that you were focused on me, but I wish you

could have seen Tiffany's face when she saw the needle in my leg. I really thought she was going to puke up those brownies her mom brought. Still would have been a better experience than suffocating on them.

You were really calm and professional through the whole thing, and I want to thank you for not making a big deal out of it (in addition to not letting me die). At least SOMEBODY on that trip read the notes section of the permission slips. Like the poster in Mrs. La Fountaine's room says, "reading can save your life." I had no idea she meant it so literally.

Thanks, again, for being cool and sticking a needle in my leg when I really needed it. You're a true friend.

Your favorite student,

Rachel

***

Dear Rachel,

Your letter gave me a good laugh this morning! You are so welcome; I am rather familiar with the need for EpiPens and "coolness" in those situations. I was highly allergic to bees as a child and have had an impressive number of people stick needles in my leg (myself included). I concur; you may want to be more cautious in accepting food from others, even adults. We are not nearly as put-together and on top of things as we would like you all to think.

I am sure Mrs. La Fountaine had the best of intentions. Unfortunately, not nearly enough people are capable of recognizing the symptoms of anaphylaxis, and even fewer know what to do when it happens. I am going to make a note at our next eighth grade group meeting that *all* of your teachers need to be aware of your condition and how to handle it properly. I'd be more than happy to give a demonstration on how to properly use an EpiPen. Would you care to join me? I have a feeling you would have no problem commanding a classroom.

Your favorite teacher,

Ms. Thompson

LITTLE NOTES FROM STUDENTS:

Dear Mr. Jones,

I want to thank you for your help teaching me and opening my mind to learning. I want to be a vet, and your help is a big help. Your funny jokes when you teach math help me so much. I did not like math, but you make it so much fun. Math is my favorite class now! Thanks for making school fun and helping me and my friends.

~*Cheyenne*, age 7

***

Dear Mom,

Thank you for hearing me. Thank you for being there when I need you the most and always having my back, especially when I have bad dreams. I know you listen when I'm stressed out about school. It is sooo important to learn, and I am thankful you hear me because without you listening, I would have never made it through the school year, because it was hard. It is important that you hear me, because you listening to me helps me a lot. Listening is important to learning.

Thank you for listening to me and what I think. It means so much to me, because it's important to hear what others have to say and to feel like people hear me.

Addison L. Guinan, 10 years old

ABOUT THE AUTHOR

Dr. Miguel Hernandez has been an eduator for over three decades and has a heart and passion for educating children and empowering teachers. Dr. Hernandez speaks, consults and coaches educators, parents and teachers and is a recognized thought leader in the education space.

www.SpeakerMiguelHernandez.com